# Ski Style

A Thomas Dunne Book.
An Imprint of St. Martin's Press.

Ski Style

Created by Co & Bear Productions (UK) Ltd.
Copyright © 2000 Co & Bear Productions (UK) Ltd.
Photographs copyright © 1999 Simon McBride.
Additional images copyright, see picture credits.

Library of Congress Cataliging-in-Publication Data

Printed and bound in Novara, Italy by
Officine Grafiche de Agostini.

ISBN 0-312-27521-8

First published in Great Britain by Scriptum Editions
First US edition: January 2001
10 9 8 7 6 5 4 3 2 1

# Ski Style

## ALPINE INTERIORS, ARCHITECTURE

## & LIVING STYLE

PHOTOGRAPHED BY SIMON MCBRIDE

WRITTEN BY ALEXANDRA BLACK

THOMAS DUNNE BOOKS / ST. MARTIN'S PRESS

NEW YORK

6

# INTRODUCTION BY WAYNE POULSEN

Skiing, in barely a century, has grown from handmade beginnings to embrace a complex range of technology and equipment, fashion and design that is unique in sport. The arrival of modern skiing can be credited to a small fellowship of visionaries who foresaw for themselves a way of life in the mountains – prophets like André Roch of Switzerland, Arnold Lunn of Great Britain and a host of young Americans. The revelation of a winter paradise was reserved for these early skiers. They strapped boards to their feet and ascended the peaks to find their reward, an intoxication in breath and blood distilled of crystal air, sun and a horizon of summits seen above the clouds.

*Ski Style* invites us to share an intimate portrait of a way of life born of sport. In these pages we are introduced to homes in the most historic ski regions: in Switzerland, in Italy and in America at Aspen, which, though more recent, has a past equally colourful. In Switzerland we find the heart of the Alpine scene. In reclusive hamlets and elegant resort towns alike, it is clear that the twentieth-century sport of skiing is not without a deeply held tradition. It is a tradition which is redolent in the beeswax-cured and coped pine panelling of a Swiss farmhouse and in the richly inscribed facade and sunny balcony of the Engadine chalet. Italy's tradition is also deep but is underpinned by Italian flair and an ancient sophistication. In Aspen we find a boom-to-bust mining town with the best of the boom still vibrantly intact, and a ski culture that has ardently grafted itself around that tradition. Whereas in the Alps we see a panoply of design growing from the traditional theme, in Aspen we discover American eclecticism. *Ski Style* encompasses both.

Building ski style employs the tradition of the hand. A society of artisans is fundamental to breathing life into the interweaving of stone and beam, fabric and decoration that makes a mountain home, and the village which enjoys this happy resource is instantly recognisable from one which does not. Yet, as this book reveals, ski style is never bound by tradition. Rather, it is inclusive: embracing technology and texture, antique arts and creative flourishes with equal passion. It has a sober mission in contending with the challenge of the mountain setting, and a glorious one in responding to the sun, the views and the active lives of skiers.

# Alpine Tradition

## St Moritz, Gstaad & Klosters

# ALPINE TRADITION

The Alps of Switzerland have long inspired awe in visitors to their peaks. In ancient times, gods were thought to dwell in the mountains; in the Romantic Age they were revered as a source of spiritual regeneration; and in modern times retreated to as a place for physical restoration, even indulgence. The country's history, way of life and arts have been shaped by this defining geographical feature, and the aesthetic style of the Alpine regions dominates the visual culture of Switzerland: in heart-shaped Lebkuchen and Edelweiss; cows and their cowbells; chocolate and cuckoo clocks; and, of course, the Alpine chalet with its stone and timber facade, small shuttered windows, low-pitched roof with wide eaves and elaborately carved beams and balconies. This type of building has changed very little over the past few hundred years, having evolved to suit its environment exactly. Whether farmhouses, mountain refuges or village houses, all are typically constructed from the timber of fir trees that swathe the lower slopes of the Alps – the closest material to hand.

For centuries these mountains, with their distinctive architecture and lifestyle, were the sole domain of the Alpine inhabitants who raised their sturdy herds on its lush meadows. The Alps have in only relatively recent times become a place where outsiders would venture. The German poet Johann Wolfgang von Goethe was one of the first visitors to fall in love with the dramatic scenery and sense of spiritual purity when he began to travel there in the 1770s. The mountain ranges of Switzerland were instrumental in shaping his understanding of nature. Other Romantics followed in his footsteps, finding

solace in the inaccessible peaks and inspiration in their beauty. Byron secluded himself in the Bernese Oberland to escape scandal in London, and there began writing his dramatic work *Manfred*. Mark Twain, Henry James, Alexandre Dumas and J. M. W. Turner were all affected. Through their novels, poems and paintings the mountains of Switzerland began to capture the popular imagination. The Alps became a romantic icon.

The logical extension of this romantic fascination was the start of tourism to the Alps. Beginning in the nineteenth century, a steady stream of European visitors journeyed to the valleys, villages and mountain slopes. At first they came in the summer: to view the fields of wild flowers, to thrive on the rarefied air, to marvel at the bare rock face of the Bernese Oberland or climb the massifs of the Engadine. Eventually, they came in winter too: for the dry, bracing cold, for the views, for ice skating, sledging and snowshoeing – and for skiing.

The origins of the ski resort can be traced to a small hotel in the village of St Moritz, set in spectacular fashion among the peaks of the Engadine above a chain of lakes that snake through the valley below. In 1864 – the same year that Thomas Cook conducted personally his first organised tour of Switzerland – innkeeper Johannes Badrutt made an intriguing offer to

OPPOSITE By the 1950s the Alpine ski resorts of St Moritz, Gstaad and Klosters had become the popular new winter destinations. Physical stimulation was part of the appeal of skiing, but equally so was the effect on mind and spirit.

RIGHT The Swiss made mountain holidays fashionable and skiing sojourns chic. The emphasis was on invigoration, pristine surroundings and old-fashioned Alpine hospitality, and the après-ski delights after a hard day on the slopes were all part of the allure.

a group of British tourists who stayed with him one summer. He would pay for their fare back and provide free lodging if they would return and stay through the winter. They would, he promised, not be disappointed. So they took him on, arriving at Christmas in a horse-drawn sleigh and remaining through the season. They sparked off a fashion for wintering in the Alps that has continued to flourish ever since. Skiing was not initially on the itinerary of those early tourists, but by the early 1900s it was firmly established as the fashionable new winter sport. By 1914, the seal was set on St Moritz as the star Swiss resort.

After World War I and the onset of the Depression, Europeans sought comfort high in the Alps. They were a place for elegant escape, but they also happened to be in tune with the mood of the times – sport and speed being the new obsessions. In 1928 the Winter Olympic Games announced to the world that St Moritz had 'arrived'. But the place had become much more than just a destination for winter sports. The luxury of chalet living was just as appealing as the skiing itself. And so it was that in the 1950s and 1960s St Moritz, and the other emerging resorts of Gstaad and Klosters, began to attract a chic, urbane clientele: thrilled by the physical sport, overwhelmed by the setting and seduced by the après-ski pleasures. Sleekly clad skiers may have boasted of their prowess on the slopes and their conquest of the mountains, but then, as now, it was the warming log fires, the sun-drenched terraces, the cosy chalets with their traditional architecture and decoration, and the prospect of finishing the day with fireside fondue and glühwein, that were the real attraction of experiencing life in the Alps.

⅋ OPPOSITE A late nineteenth-century farmhouse on a hill above Klosters was a rare
find for artist Sonya Knapp. On top of the house she has built an atelier, using local
wood so that the extension blends seamlessly with the original structure.

# NATURAL REFUGE

In Alpine resorts that are as popular, and pristine, as Klosters, trying to find a suitable home in the village is an enormous challenge. Near impossible though is the prospect of acquiring a house in the serene foothills above the town. Planning regulations all but prevent new construction and existing farmhouses tend to be held on to by the families that have lived in the valley for generations. Artist Sonya Knapp is one of the few outsiders who has managed to secure her own piece of this mountain paradise.

Knapp was living in a small apartment in the centre of Klosters but craved the isolation and space that a house would bring. Eventually she found a traditional farmhouse chalet for sale, situated high above the valley on the sunny side of Mount Gotchna. It was to become a haven into which Knapp poured heart and soul.

The house, as Knapp found it, was a single-storeyed structure dating from 1893, but needed extensive reshaping to create the working home the artist wanted. A second floor was added to give her a large and airy atelier, and the existing ground floor opened out. The restoration was expertly wrought. From the outside the additional floor looks to have been there forever, while inside the use of old timbers retains the integrity of the original house. What makes Knapp's home so intriguing is her artist's eye for colour, and her close relationship with the natural environment, including its seasonal changes. The two elements

strike a harmonious balance, a quality that is also true of Knapp's art. Canvases in progress in her atelier, and finished works on the walls of the house show the artist's talent for recording nature in her own stylised way – much influenced by Japanese aesthetics – whether floral motifs or her favourite subject, black cats.

The decoration of the house was a collaborative effort with friend and colleague Emmanuel Ungaro. He chose mainly seventeenth- and eighteenth-century English antique furnishings for their sense of solidity, and because their dark wood echoed the aged timber of the interior walls and ceilings. Having previously designed fabrics for Ungaro, Knapp shared the fashion designer's passion for colour and floral themes. They used bright kilims on the floors to add warmth and hunted out antique floral fabrics to cover sofas and cushions. Time spent in Japan inspired the sliding windows lined with shoji paper – designed to soften the strong Alpine light and eradicate the need for heavy curtains. The Japanese mood is also felt in the owner's keen affinity with seasonal changes, and use of images derived from nature.

During winter, pretty floral prints cover sofas and chairs, while bunches of dried flowers add the bright touches Knapp feels are essential in a mountain home during winter. All this changes in the summer, though, when chair coverings are swapped for plain white upholstery, and the only flowers to be seen are fresh ones. With the outdoors ablaze with brilliant greens and wild flowers, the interior looks fresh and clean – a symbolic breath of new life reflecting the changing natural world.

ABOVE & RIGHT The farmhouse is primarily
a place for creation, and the artist spends the winter
months in the top-floor atelier working on sketches, ink
paintings and sculptures. A long stint working in Japan
influenced not only her artistic style but also her living
environment. In place of curtains, Sonya Knapp has
covered windows with bamboo and paper *shoji* screens,
which soften the harsh Alpine sunlight.

↶ **LEFT** The house is intended to adapt to the seasons.
In summer, sofas and chairs are covered in white and
the rooms filled with fresh flowers. In winter, the interior
is designed to give an impression of warmth, with rich
colours and bold patterns defining the living area;
a legacy of the artist's work with Emmanuel Ungaro.

**ABOVE** Sonya Knapp is known for her stylish yet
poignant ink paintings of flowers and animals, especially
cats, which she finds the most challenging subjects.

RIGHT & BELOW In the entrance hall, a big cat rendered in ink chases a sculptured bird. Both works are by Sonya Knapp. Below the stairs, dried hydrangeas, a lamp with a rose-like stem, an antique cuckoo clock, and one of the artist's framed pastels form one of many still-life settings on floral themes.

# WINTER SOLACE

Klosters has a reputation for being one of the most rustic of the Swiss resorts. Quiet, and with a strong sense of the farming village it still is, Klosters is what the locals might call '*gemütlich*' – cosy, warm and welcoming. It is this character that attracts an entourage of semi-permanent residents, who generally live elsewhere but for years have maintained a base here; a place of escape used for all seasons. There are few, however, who can claim shares in such a special piece of the resort's architectural heritage.

Eva Beckwith has a long association with Klosters. She has been coming to the village since she was nine years old, and has always had a home of some kind here. But the one house she longed for, and walked past daily for years, seemed always out of her reach. An early seventeenth-century farmhouse set a few minutes' walk from the village centre, yet surrounded by fields, it has been in the hands of one longtime Klosters farming family for more than a century. Such properties in Klosters rarely become available to outsiders. When Beckwith heard that this particular house might be for rent she jumped at the chance to pursue it. She knew immediately that here she could create the perfect weekend base for regular escapes from the cashmere business she runs in Zürich. The space offered for rental was a large apartment on the first floor of the house, which had been converted in 1914 to provide separate living quarters for the farmer's family and his mother.

Although just five minutes'
walk away from the centre of Klosters, the farmhouse
stands in the middle of a field. In winter, a short ski
across the field leads to excellent cross-country tracks.

It was to be another few years, however, before she could take possession of the old farmhouse. With sagging floors and a thick layer of dirt over everything, it was in need of serious work. Beckwith, an interior decorator, offered to help the owners with the crucial renovations. The ancient timber floors – hanging, with no under-support – were to prove the most challenging aspect. Each of the floorboards was removed, iron beams inserted at floor level to provide a stable framework, and then each of the boards cleaned and put back in place. New electrical circuits and plumbing were installed, as well as central heating.

Even after Beckwith had moved in and decorated the farmhouse apartment, there was still one massive job to be carried out: restoring the parquetry floor in the study. Created from alternating squares of pale elm and dark maple, the chequerboard floor had become coated with layers of dirt over the years, obscuring the colour and grain of the wood. The owner of the house himself carried out the delicate operation of removing each square, numbering it, then cleaning it and returning it to the same spot. This elegant flooring seems unlikely decor for a farmhouse, but it was not uncommon for wealthy farmers to have one special room for receiving guests. It now serves as the study, while the main sitting room is more relaxed, decorated with comfortable sofas along with artworks and objects acquired over years of travels abroad. But the effect is far from cluttered. Although the rooms are infused with touches of old-world charm and hints of colonial informality, a modern restraint pervades throughout, and the sense of internal space is never sacrificed.

✿ **ABOVE & RIGHT** The sitting room is cocooned in pale honey-coloured wood which lines the ceiling, walls and floor. The apparent informality of the interior gives it great charm, as does the use of colonial-style furniture and decorative devices such as the sun hats on the wall. Furnishings have been kept low-key, focusing the attention on a few special objects and works of art including the original green porcelain *stübe*, or stove, and a Balinese painting from Ubud.

**OPPOSITE** A simple farmhouse table and bench seats form the centrepiece of the kitchen. At one end is an eighteenth-century chestnut larder from the Le Marche area of Italy, now used to store crockery and utensils.

**RIGHT & BELOW** Eva Beckwith's restrained decorative style creates wonderfully atmospheric rooms, whether the dining room with its French wrought-iron candelabra, or the master bedroom with its Balinese wicker chair and Italian appliqué bedcover.

&co OPPOSITE The vast central stairwell of the house showcases Alpine woodwork at its most extravagant. Each panel was carved in the St Moritz workshop of the renowned carpenter Romano Pedrini, before being fixed in place.

# ARTISAN BUILT

B ehind the facade of one Klosters house, built in the typical fashion of the Bernese Oberland, unfolds an interior that is unique in its interpretation of the vernacular style. It is a look that is informed by sophisticated sensibilities: a wide-ranging appreciation of art and antiques; an eclectic approach to sourcing furnishings; a love of modern proportions; an eye for subtle colouring; and a dedication to creating something very different from the expected chalet treatment of the region.

While this elegant interior would not be out of place in a Milanese villa, a London loft or a Zürich town house, it is still very much reflective of its environment in its use of Alpine materials and crafts. The owner is German but has been based in Switzerland for many years. She already had homes in St Moritz and Gstaad but was captivated by Klosters' unparalleled setting, high in the Alps. The house she found there was built in Bernese style in the 1970s, and true to tradition featured three levels of rather small rooms with heavy timber detailing.

The first step in the two-year transformation process was to strip away completely any remnants of the previous owner's layout and interior scheme. Walls were demolished and the house opened up so that on each level large airy rooms revolved around a massive stairwell. This magnificent central core is the focal point of the house, and one of its most startling

RIGHT & OPPOSITE In contrast to the massive stairwell, which doubles as a kind of art gallery, the family dining area, or *stübli*, is cosy and intimate. It is lined with antique timber and features a massive open fireplace, used for heating as well as occasional barbecues. The adjoining kitchen has its own La Cornue stove.

features; a work of art in itself. Renowned artisan Romano Pedrini, one of a handful of people who keep the Alpine woodcarving tradition alive, was brought in to create a masterpiece – a superbly carved banister that winds from floor to floor. The enormous stairwell also doubles as a kind of gallery space for a collection of modern art.

Extending Pedrini's task, the owner commissioned him to also create panels, mouldings and carved trims for the rest of the house. His expert hand is particularly evident in the expansive living area, dominated by a huge fireplace and moulded ceiling. The adjoining dining room, too, was given a symmetrically panelled ceiling. Each element was made in Pedrini's workshop in St Moritz, then transported and fitted, piece by piece, in the Klosters house.

Because Pedrini's ceilings are so beautifully wrought, they have not been compromised by the installation of light fittings. In the living and dining rooms, there are no pendant light fittings; only candelabra in the dining room and wall-mounted lights and lamps in the living room. In the daytime, however, there is no need for artificial light at all, for there are banks of windows lining the exterior walls, offering views to the mountains all around. And this explains why the owner has gone to such trouble to reinvent the house. Its position is special enough to warrant the effort. In winter, the ski slopes are five minutes' walk away, in summer hiking trails are within easy reach, and throughout the year the changing Alpine ecosystem provides a seasonal display that is visible on a panoramic scale from the comfort of the living room.

RIGHT Romano Pedrini's handiwork makes the fireplace the centre of attention in the sitting room. The carving is based on the typical motifs of the Bernese Oberland. Mixing ancient crafts with new, the room's decor includes a glass-topped coffee table with an open book as its base.

BELOW The dining table and twelve matching chairs were found in an antique shop in Paris, as were the silver candelabra. But even these fine pieces are over-shadowed by the simple geometry of Pedrini's ceiling.

 LEFT & ABOVE To create a spacious master bedroom, the original ceiling was demolished to make a loft-like space, with an intricately carved partition concealing a gallery level. The furnishing has been kept to a minimum. A huge bed piled high with silk and velvet cushions, and a gilded eighteenth-century Venetian chest of drawers contribute to a mood of modern luxury.

Ao Do 1455 VEREINIGVNG DER DREI BVENDE *
ZWISCHEN 1300 VND 1500 WIRD DER WALD
VM DAS KLOSTER GERODET VND VON DEN
WALSERN BESIEDELT * DAS KLOSTER KOMMT
VNTER DIE FREIHERREN VON MONTFORT
BIS 1477 DIE HERRSCHAFT DER HABSBVRGER

👁 OPPOSITE When American GIs were interned at the Chesa during World War II, they were enchanted by it, and returned home to spread the word about this gem of a private hotel. In the 1950s and 1960s, celebrities made it a favourite haunt.

# SWISS VIRTUE

In Klosters the honour for traditional Alpine hospitality on an intimate scale goes to the Romantik Hotel Chesa Grischuna, a picturesque chalet with a reputation as the only place in Klosters, if not to stay, then certainly to socialise. Indeed, it is credited with putting the village on the international map. In its mid-century heyday, the Chesa was something of a celebrity haunt. Audrey Hepburn, Gene Kelly, Deborah Kerr, Billy Wilder, Greta Garbo and Winston Churchill are among the names inscribed in the hotel guest book, alongside those of European royalty. Yet the hotel has remained refreshingly unaffected, perhaps because for its entire existence it has been run by a single family, the Gulers.

The Chesa began life in 1938 when a local mountain guide and ski instructor, Hans Guler, decided to open a private hotel, engaging architect Hermann Schneider to build it in the regional Grisons style. With just ten rooms, a restaurant, a bar and broad terraces for sunbathing, the Chesa was not intended to be grand. Rather, its magic lay in its snug atmosphere, Hans Guler's exacting attention to detail, and his devotion to making every guest feel part of an extended family. Numerous craftsmen and artists collaborated to produce a unique hotel interior, based on typical Grisons features, but with an individualistic flair. After Hans Guler's death in 1991, followed by that of his wife Doris in 1997, the hotel passed into the care of the couple's children, Christian and Barbara Guler, who are equally devoted to maintaining the charming Chesa tradition.

OPPOSITE & BELOW Friends of founder Hans Guler – artists and artisans – were responsible for working the decorative elements of the interior, whether wood carving or painting, all in traditional Grisons style.

RIGHT & BELOW RIGHT Bedrooms feel more like those in a private house than a hotel. Each has warm, wood details and charming individual touches that make guests feel they are staying in a family home. Beds are made up with pure linen sheets and down comforters.

⁊ OPPOSITE The American West meets Germanic tradition in the sitting room, where key furnishings and objects create a strong, clean look. By the fire, a rustic Tyrolean table supports a collection of prized nineteenth-century silver tankards.

# FRONTIER SIMPLICITY

St Moritz, arguably the most cosmopolitan of the Swiss resorts, and certainly the most extrovert, makes a logical location for what is a highly unusual home. It blends the aesthetics of not only two different cultures, but also two very different climates. Nestled high in the foothills of the mountains, with wide-reaching views, the house is built in the characteristic style of an Engadine chalet. The interior is in part inspired by the regional architecture and decoration, and in part by the rugged American Wild West, in particular Arizona, the desert state that is home to the creator of this Alpine retreat.

Elements of the house are classically Engadine: the low, timber-panelled ceiling and much of the furniture, like the painted cupboard in the bedroom, and the dining room chairs with their keyhole cut-outs. Other aspects, though, seem more informed by the American desert: the rough-hewn log lining for the bedroom, the animal horns, the whitewashed walls and a cactus garden that thrives on the mountain sunshine streaming through the windows of the living room. These two styles from opposite sides of the world combine to create a clean, chromatic masculine look. It was this that caught the attention of an Italian entrepreneur and his wife, who bought the property from its Arizona owner. The couple feel perfectly at home here, and have simply added their own stamp with family furniture from their native country.

❧ **PREVIOUS PAGE** A cactus garden in the living room creates a surreal setting for Alpine views. It was planted by the chalet's Arizonan owner to remind him of home.

**LEFT & BELOW** The Italian owners have added their own stamp to the chalet, but had no need to alter the basic interior features. The plain white walls in the living area and the simple solidity of the log-lined bedrooms provided a clean backdrop for the couple's furniture and favourite possessions.

⅋ OPPOSITE Designed to be at one with its environment, the Müller house is constructed from regional granite and timber. Using these traditional materials architect Arnd Küchel created a modern house amid 3,000 square metres of forest.

# ORGANIC FORM

On a rare plot of land in St Moritz, a modern experiment in mountain living is underway. Few residents of Switzerland's first resort have the luxury of starting from scratch on a pristine site in an exclusive residential area. It is skirted by forest, traversed by a stream for fishing in summer, and lies at the base of the Corviglia ski run, so that in winter and early spring a day's skiing begins and ends at the front door.

For Bruno and Bettina Müller and their two young daughters, this enviable location was the starting point for a holiday home planned with architectural precision. At the beginning of their search for a home in St Moritz, they engaged architect Arnd Küchel, who not only found the land but laid down the blueprint for the house and oversaw both its construction and interior fitout. Family friend and renowned Italian designer Antonio Citterio also lent his expertise to the project, and his influence is evident in the beautiful simplicity of the house.

The client brief was that the house should be built using natural materials to harmonise with the environment, and that the very layout would enable the inhabitants to feel instantly at one with the elements outside: to feel that the house was interacting with nature. Küchel devised a house built of stone from the region that comprised a three-storey tower and a connecting L-shaped wing. In the tower are a children's playroom on the ground floor, master bedroom on the level above and living room

 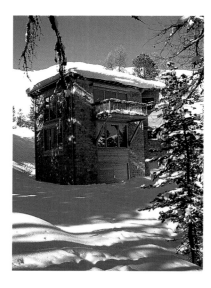

**LEFT** Encircled by fir trees, swathed in a thick blanket of snow and seemingly isolated, the house takes on an enchanted quality during the winter months.

**OPPOSITE** The traditional Swiss colours of red and white are given a modern twist in the loft-like living room with its pale ceiling of larch beams. The interior was not highly planned but evolved from this simple idea. A large white sofa scattered with checked flannelette cushions is the centrepiece of the room.

on the top level. The adjoining wing contains three bedrooms, each with its own bathroom. Each section of the house is arranged in such a way as to look directly outside to either the natural forest adjoining the property, or the mountains or garden.

Unusually for a cold-climate house, the ceilings are high and the windows are huge, with virtually no curtaining. This allows uninhibited views and gives the impression that nothing stands between the viewer and the scenic beauty beyond. The one concession to practicality is sturdy exterior wooden shutters that can seal off windows from outside elements if necessary. The chimney flue for the living room fireplace has been suspended from above, allowing an unimpeded aspect through a plate glass window to the fir trees. Even this most essential Alpine feature has been made subservient to the nature outside.

To give an impression of warmth to the large-scale interiors, reddish-gold larch wood was used for floors and for beamed ceilings, while creamy-white stucco Veneziano on the walls provided a neutral backdrop for occasional strokes of colour – like the red in the living room, or bright lavender blue in the master bedroom.

As much as possible, though, the room decor was purposely restrained, and the overall effect is one of striking simplicity. With the exception of several key pieces of modern art, there are few other distractions: no collections of local wood-carving on display, no pewter tankards, no antique memorabilia or knick-knacks; only essential furnishings and lighting. The idea is that nature provides the only aesthetic enhancement needed for this elementary, yet highly evolved, mountain residence.

RIGHT A Tricia Guild tulip print covers the
armchairs in one corner of the living room, an extension
of the red and white theme. The Müllers have built a
wooden bird house on the small terrace as a feeding
spot for birds from the forest. As many as thirty birds
at a time cluster here during winter, and bright yellow
cut-outs deter them from flying into the glass.

LEFT The master bedroom appears to be nestled in the bough of the snow-covered fir trees just outside. From the low-lying bed, the couple can look out into the forest. Decoration has been kept to a functional minimum.

ABOVE A far cry from the cosy clutter of a typical Swiss Alpine kitchen, the Müllers' cooking and eating area is streamlined and fuss-free, with an appealing Scandinavian simplicity. The focus of attention is the view across the valley to the mountains.

෩ OPPOSITE Reinforcing the idea of living in a tower, a central cupola rises up through two levels of the apartment. Celebrated woodworker Romano Pedrini crafted the columns and the beautifully inlaid floor below.

# TOWER LIVING

Rising above the lake and the old village of St Moritz, the Palace Tower is as much a part of the townscape as the backdrop of mountains, the chairlifts threading their way up to the ski runs, or the brilliant sun which St Moritz has adopted as its symbol. The tower is attached to the Palace Tower Hotel, built in 1896 as one of the first of the luxury accommodations in the emerging resort. While the hotel thrived, the tower remained largely unused until it was eventually modified to contain private lodgings, and became home to photographer and socialite Gunter Sachs in the 1960s. The most recent resident, a Swiss publisher, has perhaps brought the most dramatic change to the tower, maximising both the outlook and the structure of the tower itself.

The new tenant engaged architect Arnd Küchel to expand the existing two-bedroom apartment, occupying one floor of the tower, into a spacious four-bedroom luxury home over three floors. Intentionally designed to make the most of the views, the three-storey home is largely open-plan within the circular floor layout of the tower – arranged so that wherever one stands sweeping vistas are ever-present. This is especially so in the living area on the first level, where a dining room and cosy wood-lined *stübli* are actually alcoves within a larger living space. On the top floor, the master bedroom is ensconced within the cupola of the tower itself, in effect a luxurious lookout for observing the magnificent sweep of the Engadine Valley.

*RIGHT, OPPOSITE & BELOW* Alcoves open off the circular main living area to provide intimate spaces for dining or fireside drinks. The tiny wood-lined *stübli* is lined with magnificent cembre pine panelling, and the sofas were made in Italy especially for the room.

OPPOSITE The master bedroom occupies the top floor of the tower and the interior walls follow the lines of the tower's tapering spire. The bed, handmade by artisans in St Moritz, is positioned directly under the peak of the pyramid-shaped spire.

ABOVE LEFT & RIGHT Decorative artist Mauro Peruchetti was engaged to finish the walls in stucco Veneziano, its warm golden tones complementing the elegant but sparse furnishings. The lines of an antique Italian chaise longue are echoed by the chair at the dressing table, which can be screened off with a billowing curtain.

⅋ OPPOSITE Braquenié furnishing fabrics, based on eighteenth-century designs, are a common motif. They cover the walls and ceiling of the guest bedroom, which is dominated by an antique English bed featuring Venetian scenes.

# CHALET CHIC

To one cultured New Yorker, St Moritz is a second home. Well-travelled, erudite and with an eye for beauty, this former model turned antique dealer and interior designer has found nowhere else to match the charms of Switzerland's first resort. Its altitude means there is always plenty of snow, and its closely clustered peaks mean she can ski from mountain to mountain. In summer there is a lake for boating and swimming, horseback and hiking trails and a vibrant cultural life – and all this only two hours' travel from either Zürich or Milan.

Having vacationed in St Moritz for twenty years staying in hotels, she finally decided to establish a permanent base in an apartment in the centre of the town, within a few minutes' walk of the ski lift. On the sixth floor of a 1960s building, the apartment boasted 360-degree views, more than enough to make up for the decor – insensitive to the local tradition of architecture and craft. But there were a few fragments worth keeping. Delft tiles in the kitchen and living room were retained and used to create a fireplace surround in what is now a wood-lined open-plan kitchen and dining area. The rest of the rooms were stripped of their mid-century excess.

In place of the slick, 1960s interior emerged the cosy look of a chalet. The idea was to create the illusion of an old-fashioned Alpine home nestling high up in the mountains, despite its actual location on top of an apartment block in the centre

🚲 RIGHT & OPPOSITE A combined kitchen and dining room that would not look out of place in the chalet of the fictional Heidi. It is clad in wood reclaimed from an old Alpine house, while the Delft tiles around the fireplace are the only vestiges of the previous interior.

of St Moritz. An architect was employed along with a team of furniture makers and carpenters to help realise the two-year transformation. Reclaimed wood was found to line the kitchen and bathroom, while new wood – Engadine pine – was treated to give it an aged look and then used for panelled walls and ceilings in the living room. This renovation, though, was far from provincial. The cabinets were inlaid with marquetry by St Moritz craftsman Romano Pedrini, while luxurious fabrics and an eclectic mix of antique furnishings were used to give the interiors a sophisticated edge.

Classic French Braquenié fabrics – reproduced from eighteenth-century designs – were used to cover the walls of the living area and guest bedroom. These added instant cosiness yet were elegant enough to counter any suggestion of heaviness. The carpet was customised in Milan with colours designed to complement rather than perfectly match the wall covering. Likewise, furnishings were chosen to add interest rather than strictly harmonise. In the living room, seating was custom-built around the fireplace and windows. Ceiling and chimney decoration was based on a traditional design the owner came across while researching the apartment. Sofas and antique armchairs were covered with contrasting Braquenié fabrics.

Against this backdrop of warm tones and delicate patterns, unusual objects attest to the owner's training in the antiques business as well as her eye for the unusual. Bavarian carved reindeer, a collection of English snuff boxes, and a master bed so enormous that a room was enlarged to take it are just some of the curiosities that have come to rest in this well-bred home.

ॐ ABOVE A corner of the living room functions as a small study, centred on a colonial desk from India and an antique Russian armchair. Two unusual lamps – one with a Roman helmet for a base, the other in the form of a miniature rotunda – shed light on the desk.

LEFT Covering the walls in fabric added an instant cosiness to the living area, enhanced by characterful furnishings which include a pair of English lamps with bases fashioned from antique tea-caddies.

✃ **ABOVE** The existing plastic-framed windows in the living room were replaced with large plates of glass to give unhindered views of the mountains, making the fireside banquette a favourite place for curling up with coffee.

**RIGHT** Despite the riotous mix of patterns and fabrics, the living room feels cosy rather than overwhelming thanks to the careful choice of colour tones, the pale timber ceiling and, of course, the vast windows which flood the room with light.

&ou; OPPOSITE In the living room, upholstery in a pale, elegant pattern – based on an antique carpet from the nineteenth century – lightens the effect of the wooden panelling. A side table is topped with treasured photographs from the royal couple's collection.

# SNOWBOUND SECLUSION

In splendid isolation, the Prince Vittorio Emanuele di Savoia and his wife Princess Marina di Savoia spend their winters in a snowbound chalet just outside the village of Gstaad. From December to April they decamp from their streamlined Geneva home to this spirited, quirky and beautiful house. Surrounded by open pastureland in the shadow of the Wildhorn, and with a trout-filled river running at the foot of the garden, it is hard to imagine a more poignant setting for the descendants of Italy's exiled royal family.

Both are expert skiers and spend much of their five months here on the slopes. When not skiing, there are friends to visit, and to entertain back at their home. The chalet was built in the 1970s but with the help of interior designer Claude Reyren was completely stripped of everything but the crucial structural walls. A new floor plan was devised, centring on a large salon on the ground floor, with most of the bedrooms upstairs. Eighteenth-century boards from an old chalet were cleaned, restored and used to line the walls and ceilings of the newly defined space. Reyren has made a point of working a light, refined interior, with delicate tones used as a counterpoint to the rich honey-coloured timber. Many of the furnishings and fabrics came from France; other pieces are from northern Italy and were inherited by the prince and princess. Gifts, family portraits and memorabilia provide warm reminders of the couple's close connections with family, and with their royal heritage.

⚭ **RIGHT & BELOW** The house appears incredibly remote, surrounded by drifts of deep snow and dense stands of fir trees. It was built in the 1970s but has been renovated in the style of an old chalet.

❧ **LEFT** The entrance hall is rustic but elegant,
its floors covered with French terra-cotta tiles and the
walls lined with sisal. One wall is dominated by a
seventeenth-century tapestry of King David and
Bathsheba. An antique dresser is flanked by a pair of
antique skis, a gift to the prince, who is a ski champion.

**ABOVE** Evidence of the couple's strong family ties is
visible throughout the house and the interior designer
made sure that this element would be given prominence
in any interior scheme. In the living room, a cabinet
contains miniature portraits of royal family members.

☙ **OPPOSITE & ABOVE** The prince and princess wanted to make the tiny guest bathroom an amusing surprise for friends who came to stay. Here, they step back in time and place to late nineteenth-century France. Most of the fittings, including a remarkable copper bath, are French antiques bought in Paris.

ETAGE 0 ▽
RECEPTION
BAR

ETAGE 1 ▽
FITNESS
ACQUA-CLUB
SOLE-BAD
GARAGE

*&* OPPOSITE Now incorporated into the Grand Hotel Park, the elevator of the former Park Hotel Reuteler, with its elegant wrought-iron doors and painted figures, is typical of the decorative style of Gstaad and the Saanenland.

# GRAND DIVERSION

The Swiss *hôtel* lies at the very core of ski resort life. For decades the only type of accommodation for visitors to the mountains, the *hôtel* has gained a reputation for the warmth of its hospitality; for the homely charm of its interior style; and for distilling to perfection the essence of Alpine living. It was here that the first nineteenth-century tourists came to stay for their summer sojourns to the mystic Alps; where early skiers learned their new sport; and around which even today the social life of many mountain villages revolves. The Alpine hoteliers of Switzerland have come to pride themselves on the unique environment they have created for guests to appreciate mountain living in winter – a melding of personal warmth and efficiency, of dramatic views outside and cosy *stüblis* inside.

In the Bernese Oberland, the town of Gstaad is known for cultivating a rather more rarefied image than other ski resorts, and this is reflected in its elegant hotels. In particular, the Grand Hotel Park has evolved the Swiss tradition of Alpine hospitality, and of the Alpine 'cure', into a refined art. Built in the chalet style of the former Park Hotel Reuteler, which it superseded, with quaint carved balconies giving panoramic views, the Grand Hotel Park recreates the discreet luxury of a late nineteenth-century Alpine hotel. Pale oak wood panelling, antiques of the Bernese Oberland and charming remnants of the old hotel evoke the early days of travel to the Swiss Alps, when it was the most fashionable of destinations.

BELOW & RIGHT Although a relatively recent structure, the Grand Hotel Park is built in traditional chalet style, in accordance with the strict planning regulations that preserve the architectural integrity of Gstaad. Inside too, long-practised crafts in wood-carving, iron work and rustic painting conjure up the ambience of past elegance.

⅋ OPPOSITE The living room of this mid-seventeenth-century farmhouse keeps alive the handicraft traditions of Gstaad. The massive carved balcony was added some time after the original construction and now conceals a library on the gallery level.

# MODERN FOLKLORE

Photographer and former industrialist Gunter Sachs was a young man at university when he began what has become a longstanding relationship with Gstaad. Studying at Lausanne he would often spend weekends and holidays skiing in nearby Gstaad with friends. He admits it may have been a sense of nostalgia, the longing to return to a place where idyllic days were spent, that drew him back there many years later.

Memories of student days aside, it is not hard to see what attracted Sachs to the seventeenth-century farmhouse, which he shares with his wife Mirja. The house dates from the mid-1600s, when it was built by a peasant farmer whose cows grazed over much of what is now Gstaad. From his home, perched on a hill, he could survey his herds, and the surrounding mountains. Sachs has enjoyed the same aspect for more than twenty-five years, over that time transforming the property into a small estate. In addition to the substantial farmhouse, with its typical dark timber facade and rows of tiny shuttered windows with flower boxes, the site now supports a separate, self-contained guest cottage as well as a lavish pool house with bar and billiard room.

Respect for the traditions of Gstaad has led Sachs to decorate his living environment largely with folk arts and furnishings of the region. He wanted it to reflect the landscape and the Alpine aesthetics of the area but not to the extent of slavishly

🐛 RIGHT & OPPOSITE There are several dining areas in the house: the terrace provides the perfect spot for daytime meals with a view. Shearling-covered seating by a huge roaring fire makes the ideal place to curl up after meals and relax. The fireplace was brought here from a seventeenth-century castle in Burgundy.

replicating the established chalet conventions. Instead, he has interpreted the look in his own particular fashion, mixing sombre tones with bright colours, rough textures with luxurious ones and ancient arts with pop art. In doing so, the enigmatic Sachs has imbued the interior of his farmhouse with a distinctive modern edge.

Given Sachs' extraordinary life in the limelight, it is not surprising that his home incorporates an element of the dramatic. The heir to the Sachs and Opel fortune, Sachs was married to Brigitte Bardot, counted the Kennedys among his friends, and established a reputation for his bold, stylised photographic art. Indeed, his work makes a strong visual statement throughout the Gstaad house, in bedrooms, and in public spaces, like the anteroom where two large starkly modern portraits are points of contrast in the otherwise traditional setting with its stone paved floor, whitewashed walls and dark timber furniture.

In the barn-like living room, where the original peasant owner and his family would once have slept, all is now sensual indulgence. Enveloping sofas and low-level seating are covered in a thick layer of lambswool, while a massive stone fireplace generates heat throughout the winter, making this a hedonist's lair – almost primitive in its mix of animal skins, stone and wood. In other rooms the interior scheme swings from handcrafted earthiness through rustic elegance to modern luxury. It is in the pool house that Sachs has unleashed his flamboyant side. Here an aquatic dreamscape unfolds, as swimming pool, hanging gardens and trompe-l'oeil forest combine to create a setting fit for any playboy fantasy.

🚲 **PREVIOUS PAGE** Photographs by Gunter Sachs transform a simple anteroom with its slate floors, white walls and peasant furniture into a modern gallery.

**LEFT & BELOW** In a gallery above the swimming pool perches the den, an intriguing mix of 1960s styling and traditional craft. The eighteenth-century ceiling was rescued from a town hall in the village of Zerenz, near St Moritz. In contrast, the Warhol images of Sachs' former wife, Brigitte Bardot, and the low-slung sofa recall the 1960s. Sachs designed the pool house as a place of fantasy, commissioning Austrian artist Wolfgang Ploner to render a trompe-l'oeil forest at one end, and a pale blue sky overhead.

ABOVE The master bedroom with its textured white carpet, folkloric-print wallcovering, painted wardrobe and patchwork quilt is sweetly naive.

RIGHT Like most of the furniture in the farmhouse, this carved nineteenth-century peasant trunk in the master bedroom is a typical craft of Gstaad and the surrounding Saanenland region.

# ITALIAN DRAMA

## CORTINA & THE DOLOMITES

# ITALIAN DRAMA

I t is true to say of all ski resorts that their atmosphere, character and aestheticism are dictated by the precise nature of the mountains surrounding them, affecting the views, the climate, the lifestyle and the forces that have shaped skiing culture. Nowhere is this more so than in Cortina d'Ampezzo. Nestled in a broad sunny basin, this picturesque northern Italian town is surrounded by the jagged peaks of the Dolomites, an ancient mountain range that has given Cortina a unique appeal.

Thirty million years ago, as powerful geological forces were shaping the Alps of central Europe, another equally dramatic event was taking place on their southern frontier. Ancient Triassic sediments, comprising a unique combination of dolomitic and volcanic rock, were being pushed up to create the Dolomites. These sheer cliffs rise not to the ordered, triangular peaks of the Alps but finish in jagged shards and ragged blocks, as though still not fully formed. There is something almost prehistoric about their form that only serves to emphasise the fragile beauty of the town of Cortina: the charming Tyrolean chalets, the elegant spire of its romantic Renaissance church, piazzas lined with frescoed villas and pale stucco facades.

The attraction of this area is by no means new. In the valleys and on the foothills cling villages that served as stopovers for medieval travellers passing through the empire of the Counts of Tyrol, who had absorbed this formerly Roman enclave. In 1363, the House of Hapsburg acquired the Tyrol lands, and the Hapsburgs were entranced by Cortina cradled in its sunny basin, and made it their favourite holiday destination. It was a privilege that was to last for centuries, only briefly interrupted when the

RIGHT Italians began avidly ski-holidaying in Cortina in the 1930s, lured by the rugged scenery and sunny disposition of the Dolomites, which form a giant suntrap.

Republic of Venice took control in the fifteenth century. Cortina came to the popular attention of Austria in 1877, when the Viennese climber Paul Grohmann published an account of his adventures in the Dolomites. This, along with several books on the region by British mountaineers and the completion of a new railway, helped to establish Cortina as a tourist destination largely for British, Austrians and Germans. Then, in the wake of World War I, national borders were redrawn, and Cortina, along with the Dolomites, became part of Italy.

The villages of the Dolomites now reflect the aesthetics and traditions of their Tyrolean heritage and their more recent Italian history. This intermingling is visible in the building style, in crafts and decorative arts, in the food and lifestyle. The chalets, like those in the Alps, are made from local timber with broad decks to catch the sun, decorative carving and deep eaves. They have also inherited a characteristically Italian flair, which affects not only the approach to decoration, but to living and leisure.

Skiing came somewhat later to Cortina than it did to the rival Swiss resorts, but of any of the European resorts, Cortina has raised the skiing lifestyle to a fine art. For a start it has been endowed with a great natural advantage – during the day there is almost always sunshine. Even in winter skiers are assured of seven hours' sunlight a day. And for all but the most rigorous of the ski fraternity, the sun is as important to ski life as the snow itself.

CORTINA
m.1200-2500

All Winter Joys

**OPPOSITE & RIGHT** Following the occupation of Cortina during World War II, the town quickly recovered its appeal. By 1950 it was once again attracting Italian families for ski holidays. The same year it was the site of the international bobsled competition, and in 1956 it hosted the Winter Olympics, which was to prove a turning point.

The sun made Cortina a magnet for pleasure-loving Italians. From the early 1920s wealthy entrepreneurs, the nobility and the literary and artistic set began travelling to Cortina in the summer. Over the next four decades Cortina built a reputation as an Alpine sporting centre, attracting mainly Italians but also a handful of foreigners, among them Ernest Hemingway and Aldous Huxley. Farmers' houses were bought up and redecorated to provide romantic holiday retreats for these converts to mountain life. But largely the resort's charms were a well-kept secret outside of Italy until the 1956 Winter Olympics, when it made an impressive international debut.

In the 1960s, Cortina blossomed into a resort of jet-setting calibre, where the skiing itself was almost incidental. Much as they do now, holidaymakers made a leisurely start to the day, venturing down to Lovat for hot chocolate and Krapfen pastries, before deciding on which sunny slope to venture by cable car for a morning ski. Lunch on a panoramic mountain terrace working on their tans was followed by a ski down into the town for a change of dress and an afternoon of shopping. Strolling the boutiques of the Corso Italia were baronesses and marchesas in their fur coats and big hair, models and actresses in their ski pants and goat hair boots. Elizabeth Taylor, Audrey Hepburn, Henry Fonda or Cary Grant might even have been glimpsed. The glamour of Cortina became, and still is, undeniably seductive. And the indulgence of après-ski life, at which the village excels, is made even more delicious by the silent, austere presence of the rugged Dolomites.

*❧* OPPOSITE The key to the tasteful decoration of Roberto Memmo's Cortina home lies in its mix of genteel touches and antique objects, set against the backdrop of rustic timber and stone that were used to construct the eighteenth-century house.

# RESTORATION JEWEL

I t is appropriate that a man renowned for his generous support of Italy's architectural treasures should himself lay claim to two of Cortina's most historic buildings. On Via Roma, within view of the town's campanile and Piazza Venezia, these two adjacent buildings have been linked to form an expansive and gracious winter residence.

Philanthropist Roberto Memmo is founder of the Foundation Memmo, responsible for the restoration of Rome's magnificent Palazzo Ruspoli, among its many projects. He had spent many seasons in Cortina, staying in hotels, when a property came on the market that his artistic inclinations could not resist. It was a prime site in the heart of the town that included two neighbouring structures. One was a barn and stables dating from 1700; the other a former bishop's house built in 1860 when the province was part of Austria. In 1918 the house had served as a fortress against the onslaught of Italian forces who entered World War I against Austria, but the following year the Treaty of St Germain established a new border, placing Cortina and the bishop's house in Italy.

Memmo engaged the legendary architect Luigi Vietti, credited with some of the most impressive conversions in Cortina, to work with him in creating a home on the historic site. Vietti's trademark was his ability to combine a respect for traditional architectural forms and the environment with an ultimately modern sensibility. It was with this skill that he set about

LEFT Unusual objects and pockets of visual interest add great character to the house, whether a display of rare eighteenth-century wine glasses or an old fireplace niche filled with red candles.

OPPOSITE The original doors of the old house did not survive. Instead, the owner installed antique doors – each of the doors to the bedrooms is different.

transforming both barn and house into a workable whole; a process that took three years. Interestingly, it is the older of the two buildings that now has an unexpectedly contemporary look. This may be due to the large loft that is the heart of the barn – essentially one open space under a pitched, beamed roof which once sheltered farm animals and hay – or it may be a result of combining new and old objects. Contemporary, low-level, custom-made sofas are clustered around a large coffee table with ferns sprouting from its centre, serving as a relaxed area for the family to unwind. In contrast, a rustic whitewashed hearth and chimney are adorned with angelic motifs and mirrors, while displays of primitive and antique objects are arranged with a modern sense of texture, colour and dramatic impact.

Connecting the old barn to the nineteenth-century house is a medieval-style corridor, leading to the refined rooms of the former bishop's residence. Twelve bedrooms with bathrooms and an exquisitely decorated living and dining area create an almost palatial atmosphere. This is the only venue in Cortina grand enough to host the annual ski club dinner for 250 guests.

Roberto Memmo's discriminating eye is evident in every room. His exquisite collection of antique tapestries depicting biblical scenes is a theme that connects the many rooms of the house. Fittingly for a home that was built in what was once Austria, it has a distinctly Tyrolean feel. This is reflected in romantic lace bedcovers, in rich red velvet sofas and in the aged timber that lines ceilings and walls, sourced long ago from the forests of the Counts of Tyrol.

ABOVE & RIGHT The formal sitting room and adjoining dining room date from 1700. A gilded green Austrian ceramic stove from the late eighteenth century dominates the sitting room, while in the dining room an eighteenth-century church organ from the nearby Val Pusteria takes pride of place. A pair of black ladies' bonnets from the nineteenth-century hang on one wall.

✿ LEFT A vaulted hallway connects the eighteenth-century farm building with the nineteenth-century house. Architect Luigi Vietti was responsible for masterminding the linking and restoration of both parts of the current property.

ABOVE Guarding the entrance to the formal sitting and dining area are two lifesize Indian soldiers. They are made from wood and date from the nineteenth century.

LEFT & ABOVE A large open-plan living room occupies the top floor of the old farm building. Where hay might once have been stored during the winter months, the Memmo family now relax by a monumental fireplace flanked by antique angels. Windows set into the eaves of the loft allow superb views to the mountains.

✣ BELOW & RIGHT Architect and interior designer
Luigi Vietti's trademark style is evident in the informal
dining room. A long wooden table is edged on one side
with banquette seating. The simplicity of the setting, the
symmetrical arrangement of objects, the flickering yellow
candles and the presence of a saintly icon give this
room a charged atmosphere that is close to medieval.

𝆕 OPPOSITE A sun-drenched balcony provides views to Mount Tofana. The ski slopes are just ten minutes' walk away. Thanks to the work of architect Luigi Vietti, the house belies its 1960s origins, conveying the character of an old chalet.

# SKI ROMANCE

The late architect Luigi Vietti was something of a Cortina institution. He worked all over Italy, particularly in Sardinia where he designed for the Aga Khan's island resort, Costa Smeralda, but he is especially respected for his Alpine work in Cortina, which shows an expert understanding and use of indigenous techniques and materials. Vietti himself lived in the mountains of Cortina for many years, arriving in the years before World War II and living there on and off for the rest of his life. During that time he was prodigious, establishing a signature style that was much sought after for its relaxed charm. He worked on many Cortina homes, but in one in particular he has wrought perhaps his most romantic mountain interior.

Vietti was commissioned to split a large family house into four self-contained apartments for various members of the extended family. One of the owners, a property developer who had worked with Vietti on many projects, was to have the top apartment for himself and his immediate family. His brief to Vietti was to respect the mountain chalet tradition of the Dolomites, using materials sympathetic to the locale. At the same time, though, Vietti wanted to make the house a new one, so that while the design would be evocative of the classic chalet, it would also have a contemporary sensibility, suited to modern family life, and arranged to make the most of the wonderful views. This meant building generously sized rooms instead of cosy chalet ones,

**RIGHT** As in Cortina chalets of old, lacy white curtains add romance, as well as providing contrast with the wooden panelled walls and beamed ceiling.

**OPPOSITE** Although part of the open-plan living area, the dining corner has an intimate feel, thanks to lace-trimmed windows, shelves of antique brass, pewter and porcelain and silver candelabra fitted with red candles.

with high ceilings instead of low, and big windows instead of tiny ones to take advantage of magnificent views. To that end, the top level was partitioned to create three bedrooms and a large L-shaped, open-plan living room with galleried loft, featuring a huge expanse of windows looking out to Mount Tofana. The interior walls in one section of the living room were given a coat of white stucco – true to local tradition. Much of the rest of the apartment was lined in thick panels of local spruce wood, treated to give it the colour and patina of age.

The decor is rustically romantic. In keeping with Italian Alpine convention, collections of antique pewter and porcelain are displayed on shelves and side tables. An eighteenth-century porcelain wood-burning stove adds an authentic Tyrolean touch, and creates the focal point for a secluded seating area in one corner of the living room. But the main feature of the home is an enormous sofa, designed by Vietti with plump, deep red cushions within a long, low sweeping frame. It takes centre stage in the living room, and is positioned in front of a wall of windows that frame the mountains.

As a counterpoint to the wood-lined walls, bright splashes of red upholstery, delicate lace and vintage embroidery lend visual warmth and old-fashioned comfort to the open-plan interior spaces. During the day, the Dolomites rise in spectacular fashion beyond the apartment, while at night, the flicker of candles and a roaring fire in the grate bring a sense of enchantment and timelessness to this most appealing of Cortina chalets.

**❧ LEFT & ABOVE** The open lounge and dining area were designed by Vietti to provide a functional and accessible living environment for the family. He also designed the long red velvet sofa to suit the layout. The room is artfully divided into a number of different spaces without the need for interior walls. An intimate sitting area in one corner, lined with books, prints and paintings, is clustered around an open fire. Above the fireplace hangs an early twentieth-century watercolour by Squittieri.

**ABOVE RIGHT** The focal point of the cosy *stübli* is a ceramic stove that was reproduced from an eighteenth-century Venetian design.

❧ OPPOSITE From the window of her Cortina apartment, decorated in the style of an elegant Austrian chalet, Donatella Girombelli can survey the Dolomite mountains that for centuries belonged to the Counts of Tyrol and the Hapsburg empire.

# TYROLEAN CHARMS

Cortina's Austrian heritage is prized by many of the resort's most discerning inhabitants, its rather austere aestheticism in sharp contrast to the embellishment typical of much Italian decoration. When Donatella Girombelli was looking for a winter home in Cortina she rejected the idea of a luxurious Italian-style villa or apartment, and opted instead for something more discreet – a chalet with a truly Austrian flavour.

The house she found was built in the 1950s and decorated by its last owners in the modern style of the period. To convert this lacklustre premises into the Tyrolean chalet of her dreams, Girombelli turned to decorator Daniela Leusch, who embarked on a two-year renovation that first entailed gutting every remnant of the existing interior.

The most significant step in the transformation was to line the walls, ceiling and floor with pine wood, in the style of an eighteenth-century Austrian chalet. Leusch found the perfect fit in an old chalet scheduled for demolition in neighbouring Val Pusteria. She bought up the aged wood inside and transferred it to Girombelli's chalet, instantly stamping the interior with a Tyrolean feel. The furnishings were kept simple and practical, yet comfortable, the sofas and chairs covered in a rich red velvet. The decorator scoured local antique shops and markets in Salzburg to find a few special pieces for the finishing flourishes: a collection of precious pewter vessels, a northern Italian bureau and a splendid eighteenth-century chandelier from Austria.

OPPOSITE Clusters of typically Austrian decorative objects, like these gleaming pewter bowls and canisters, help to conjure up the atmosphere of a Tyrolean chalet.

FAR LEFT, LEFT & BELOW The patina and tone of antique timber, whether in doors, panelled walls or antique Alpine furniture, is an essential part of the character of this visually rich apartment. Much of the old pine wood came from the interior of a chalet in the neighbouring Val Pusteria.

LEFT & BELOW A rich red is the key interior colour in the main living area, and in the master bedroom, taking its cue from the red velvet upholstery fabric that interior designer Daniela Leusch stumbled upon while travelling in St Moritz. It is the same velvet used by Swiss railways to cover the seats in its train carriages. Touches of white lace lighten the mood.

❧ OPPOSITE Designer Alda Fendi's home serves as a mountain refuge, a place for escaping the pressures of work. Here, she envelops herself in the natural beauty of the Dolomites and in the history of Tyrolean decorative arts.

# DESIGNER EMPIRE

Students of the material culture of Cortina and the eastern Dolomites would be well advised to examine the home of designer Alda Fendi. They would not find a quaint chalet or a rustic farmhouse but a compact apartment that has been transformed into a melting pot of Tyrolean and Italian influence.

In her customised mountain refuge, she has achieved a lush symbiosis of Italian passion and Germanic propriety, of nineteenth-century Austrian craftsmanship and Roman flair. The starting point for the designer's home came at the end of a holiday in Cortina, when she was taken to see two cramped top-floor apartments in the town. The rooms were small and poorly laid out, the decor was drab and uninviting, but the views were magical. Fendi bought the properties without further consideration.

Perhaps it is not surprising that a designer with the clout and reputation of Alda Fendi could see potential so readily in an apparently uninspiring property, nor that she knew instinctively just how it should be changed. Proof of her conviction came with the speed at which she completed the renovation. Just a year after she had found them, the two apartments had been opened up, redesigned and decorated to form a single residence, a holiday retreat for herself, her husband and two children. From virtually the moment of purchase, Fendi had decided that the theme for the interior would be nineteenth-century

✿ RIGHT & OPPOSITE Taking nineteenth-century Biedermeier furniture as their starting point, Alda Fendi and interior designer Cesare Rovatti have together created a tasteful home that, while essentially historical, is also welcoming and comfortable.

Biedermeier – the German furniture style renowned for its purity of form. Interior designer Cesare Rovatti, a longtime associate, shared her enthusiasm and together they began visiting Rome antique dealers to help them source the right pieces from Austria.

Meanwhile, local craftsmen were employed to install the interior detailing – wooden panelling and exquisitely carved cornicing – all a tribute to the enduring artistic skills of the mountain communities in the Dolomites. Layered over are rich fabrics covering walls, floors and furnishings – paisleys, dark red velvet, tapestries and Turkish carpets convey a sense of late nineteenth-century opulence, against which the Biedermeier furnishings appear beautifully streamlined. The obsession with the decorative arts of the Biedermeier period is evident on a smaller scale too, and Fendi has proved an avid collector of all things relating to the style: cabinets, side tables, glassware, ornamental porcelain and silverware.

The designer's tasteful take on Alpine living reflects a romantic approach to decoration. Where her profession depends on change and innovation, at home she prefers the perennial appeal of historical reference. Certainly her Cortina home is intended to provide a complete break from work, a retreat where she can relax, enjoy long afternoon teas, play cards and watch the changing mountainscape. But even more than this, Fendi considers her home a place of entrancement. It was, after all, the light of the Dolomites – filtering through windows nestled high in the eaves – that first captured her imagination, and its ethereal quality has guided the designer on her quest to make this a home not only of style, but of passion.

**LEFT & ABOVE** Lined with paisley fabrics in a rich colour palette and trimmed with flounces, frills and lace, the bedrooms are undeniably romantic. Alda Fendi has deftly transformed the rooms to thoroughly eradicate any trace of the original drab interior scheme.

❧ **ABOVE** The breakfast nook with its pine-panelled walls, paisley-covered banquettes and plump petit-point cushions is a focal point for family life. Framed paintings of farmyard chickens and a matching tea set create a relaxed, rustic atmosphere.

**OPPOSITE** In a compact guest bathroom, the Biedermeier theme is taken to its logical conclusion with a streamlined pedestal basin and slender mirror.

✽ OPPOSITE The kitchen with its rough stone walls and peasant furniture attests
to the origins of this eighteenth-century farmhouse. The owner has remained true to
the spirit of the house with a collection of colourful provincial pottery from Italy,
colonial America, Morocco and Mexico.

# FARMHOUSE RETREAT

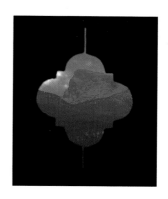

Alpine wood, cut from the pines of the Dolomites, has been used to build chalets in Cortina for hundreds of years. Its warm, golden-brown hue and patina of age are almost impossible to replicate with modern materials. Much of it was stripped from chalets and farmhouses during the 1950s and 1960s when they were converted into modern flats. As a result, this antique wood has become highly prized by home owners in the resort, many of whom have gone to great lengths to acquire it from an old house due to be demolished, transferring it length by length to its adopted home.

Only a dozen or so residents in Cortina are fortunate enough to live in properties untouched by modernisation. Publisher Leonardo Mondadori is one of them, and is not blind to his good fortune – perhaps because he spent two decades waiting for it. Mondadori has been visiting Cortina regularly since the age of two. He was twenty-five when he first saw the house that was eventually to become his mountain retreat. He mentally earmarked it as his own, but it was not until some twenty years later that his ski instructor introduced him to a friend who suggested a way to make the dream reality.

The large eighteenth-century farmhouse stood on the outskirts of town, commanding views across the valley to Mount Tofana. Owned by the church – a gift from a parishioner who died without heirs – it was close to ruin, but the church lacked the

LEFT Snowy expanses surround the farmhouse during the winter months, allowing the owner plenty of opportunities for skiing and snowshoeing.

OPPOSITE The hay loft is now a relaxed, open living room for entertaining friends. The idea was to create a welcoming space that was not in the least bit imposing. Low seating areas were formed with soft, crimson wool sofas that are more like mattresses in style.

funds to fix it. Mondadori approached them with an offer they couldn't refuse. He would undertake the costly task of fully restoring the property in return for a long lease granting him right of residency.

Underpinning the house was the first priority to prevent its imminent collapse. A team of craftsmen then spent two years restoring and rebuilding every feature, from the roof to the floorboards. In order to re-use the original interior wood, every plank was dismantled, cleaned and then reassembled. Once the structure had been completely refurbished, Mondadori turned to its decoration, commissioning Rome-based interior designer Verdi Visconti.

With its large, wood-lined rooms and massive beamed ceilings, the house had such a strong personality that it required decorating with a restrained hand. Visconti concentrated on solid, streamlined furnishings, modern blocks of colour, discreet lighting and monumental pieces of art to achieve the desired effect. She avoided the romantic patterning and heavily textured Tyrolean-style of interior so typical elsewhere in Cortina.

The end result of Visconti's considered eye and Mondadori's unpretentious tastes is a house of great character. It has an eclectic quality that accommodates both the rough and refined. Uneven stone walls and smoothly polished floors; Julian Schnabel canvases and provincial ceramics; farmhouse furniture and Mondadori's own extraordinary handmade Gothic bed sit together with equal ease. None of these disparate elements, however, distract from the integrity of the historic structure itself.

OPPOSITE A formal dining room now occupies the former feed stalls for the farm animals. The table and fourteen chairs were made in provincial style to suit the rustic quality of the room. The horn chandelier was found in an antique shop near Cortina.

LEFT & BELOW Leonardo Mondadori is an avid collector of pottery, ceramics and rustic utensils. In the kitchen they strike just the right note, adding interest without compromising the beautiful austerity of the room.

**PREVIOUS PAGE** Set away from the town of Cortina, the house enjoys unhindered views of farmland, forest and the jagged peaks of Le Cinque Torri.

**ABOVE & RIGHT** The master bedroom and ensuite bathroom are encased in antique knotted pine. Almost filling the bedroom is a fifteenth-century Gothic bed, which was reassembled in the room piece by piece.

OPPOSITE The original stove has been retained in a corner of the dining room, making it one of the warmest spots in the house. In times past, a platform above the stove provided a place for sleeping.

LEFT & BELOW The bathrooms are charmingly earthy in character. The handcrafted wooden bathtub was inspired by the traditional Japanese *o-furo*.

ABOVE & RIGHT The historic house has such a
strong personality that owner Leonardo Mondadori
wanted to keep any decoration to a minimum. He has
even retained the original layout of the house, one of
the few in Cortina to have survived intact for several
centuries. The wood lining this small sitting room has
also survived – its rich patina required little embellishment to create a cosy place for informal meals.

# THE WILD WEST

ASPEN, COLORADO

# THE WILD WEST

For the Ute Indians, the valley of Roaring Fork – encircled by mountains impassable to those not familiar with every twist of the Roaring Fork River – was an essential stop on their seasonal migrations. This was the Indians' summer hunting grounds, a place they called Shining Mountains. To the miners who navigated Independence Pass in 1879 in the hopes of finding gold or silver, it held promise of a different kind. But even the most ambitious of the gold-rushers could not fail to be impressed by the grandeur of what would one day be known as Aspen. The miners were the first recorded skiers here. To help them get around in the thick powder snow, they fashioned primitive cross-country skis – a skill learnt from the Scandinavian miners – to propel them across the surface of the deep winter snows, from their claims up in the foothills down to the fledgling township for supplies. But they can't have failed to get a thrill from coasting over crisp, newly fallen snow in the muffled silence of a sunny winter's morning. It wasn't long before ski races were inaugurated to amuse the town's new citizens during the long winter – just one of many outdoor pursuits that were to become a preoccupation of modern-day Aspenites.

As the silver mines began to yield what would be one of the biggest silver lodes in history, Aspen grew to match the newfound prosperity. The first roughly constructed wooden shacks were replaced by more substantial multi-storey shingle houses and commercial buildings. By the end of the nineteenth century many of these had been replaced by impressive Victorian-style buildings of brick and tile, even an opera house and one of America's most luxurious hotels, the Jerome,

complete with private bathrooms, electricity and an elevator. Aspen had arrived. No matter how impressive the town's facilities,

though, it was the setting, the exhilarating sight of mountains rising all around, that seduced all but the most hardened mining

man. But the euphoria was short-lived. The silver market crashed almost as suddenly as it had surged, leaving Aspen in its wake

to recover. The miners packed up and left. The businesses that served them floundered, and the Hotel Jerome, built in splen-

dour to serve the town's wealthy visitors, stood empty. Those who remained, together with a handful of newcomers, turned to

ranching to sustain them while the town slumbered.

In 1945 industrialist Walter Paepcke and his wife Elizabeth visited Aspen and hit upon a plan that was to prove the town's

salvation. They would build a ski lift and reinvent the failed mining centre as a world-class ski resort. The following year Walter

Paepcke inaugurated Aspen's first ski lift, the world's longest. Just three years later, Aspen became the first resort in America

to host an international competition, the World Alpine Championships.

Paepcke's timing was impeccable. The prosperous post-war years had given Americans a new lifestyle. They had leisure

time, and money to spend on it. Fitness and sport were new obsessions, and skiing came to encapsulate the optimistic

young America in tune with nature. Americans flocked to Aspen to discover the Alpine perfection of Europe combined with a

distinctly Colorado flavour and a sunny disposition. There was something more, too. Hand-in-hand with the boom in skiing was

a cultural renaissance that elevated Aspen above other picturesque ski resorts of the American West. With its music and film festivals, its Physics Institute, its art galleries and its historic architecture, Aspen became a creative hub attracting alternative and artistic minds, feeding off a setting that never fails to inspire. In her book *Aspen: Dreams and Dilemmas*, Peggy Clifford summarised its appeal: 'Aspen's dazzling setting, its freewheeling style, its originality, its clever mix of art and sport made it singularly desirable. Because it was out of step, it was in vogue …

Aspen became trend-setting: It was here that the fashion for stretch ski pants was kick-started, that the first quilted jackets appeared on the slopes, and that freestyle skiing gained a foothold. It attracted sophisticates and ski bums. It also attracted its share of celebrities – Gary Cooper, Hunter S. Thompson, Jack Nicholson and John Denver. Anyone who was anyone in America wanted to be seen in Aspen.

In the 1960s and 1970s, land was still cheap in Aspen and the dream of living there was open to all. In the days before planning regulations, they were free to build as the land inspired – using timber and stone from the mountain foothills, or in the classic European chalet style, or a combination of both. What was common to all who came then – and to others who have followed in their wake, whether in modern condominiums or restored Victorian mansions – was a respect for the mountains, and an unfettered passion not only for skiing, but also for the ski lifestyle.

🐇 OPPOSITE A large, south-facing dining room offers panoramic views of Aspen's mountains. The interior is partially lined with spruce, emitting a sweet subtle smell that infuses the cabin with the scent of the woods outside.

# CABIN FEVER

On the south side of Aspen Mountain, on what its owner describes as one of the most beautiful sites in America, is a property that follows in the tradition of the mountain shelters of Alpine Europe. It is a small chalet, built by hand using timber and stone from the surrounding land by local architect Wayne Poulsen. Most of his work is in mountain settings, and his expertise in designing structures attuned to their location is evident here.

Poulsen spent four years building his cabin by hand out of massive logs cut from spruce trees on the ten-acre site, which was once a mining claim. All his experience of mountain architecture and his passion for Aspen's ski country have gone into it. It is built in the style of a late nineteenth-century Swiss chalet. But unlike the wooden chalets of Switzerland, with their neat windows encased by shutters, Poulsen's house incorporates vast walls of glass looking out onto a pristine, sun-drenched mountain landscape. The wonderfully temperate Aspen climate, with bright skies through most of the winter months, means that more heat is trapped by allowing the sun into the house than is lost through the expanses of glass. This feature also gives the home a strong connection with its wild and isolated setting.

Inside, the cabin is simple and comfortable, dominated by the solid spruce logs and their subtly sweet aroma. They form a canopy over the large main room, which comprises a south-facing living area with adjoining dining space and kitchen.

FAR LEFT As it is only a twenty-minute drive by snowcat from Aspen town, the cabin can be used as a day base for skiing off-piste.

LEFT & OPPOSITE Architect Wayne Poulsen built his cabin himself, from logs hewn from trees that had fallen or died on the surrounding acreage. He was inspired by the traditional art of building mountain shelters.

A bedroom, bathroom and sleeping loft complete the compact mountain retreat. It is furnished in sturdy Alpine style. A giant sleigh bed provides fireside seating, and the long dining table is made from solid logs joined in classic Alpine fashion.

Poulsen's thousand-square-foot cabin provides ample space for his weekend ski getaways. A twenty-minute drive from his main home and architectural practice in Aspen town takes him to the chalet door, along a dirt road that winds up the back side of Aspen Mountain. Once a miners' access track, it can only be navigated by snowcat during the long winter months. A short foray further up the mountain puts him directly on the piste.

Although originally intended as an upscale ski hut, providing instant access to the slopes, it has become much more. Poulsen often finds himself here during the week, just to spend the day, or to cook dinner for friends. The enormous French-style central fireplace is utilised for informal suppers, cooked on a grill over the open fire, and if guests want to stay over, there is plenty of room in the galleried sleeping loft. In summer, when the cultural activities in town are in full swing, Poulsen hosts a private piano festival, performing on his grand piano and inviting friends to play.

Despite the undoubted charms of the cabin in summer, when wild flowers carpet the fields outside and the sky stays light until late into the evening, it really comes into its own in winter. Then, the vast snowy landscape outside serves only to emphasise the warmth of the fire inside and the gentle scent of spruce that fills the cabin.

TOP, ABOVE & RIGHT When friends arrive for mid-week ski parties or weekend soirees, they gather around the huge fireplace, perching on fireside cushions or curling up on the Norwegian-style sleigh bed. The galleried loft upstairs provides ample sleeping space. During summer, the grand piano takes pride of place when Poulsen hosts his own private music festival.

ABOVE & OPPOSITE As the cabin is often used for entertaining, most of the space is given over to an open-plan kitchen and dining area. To make the most of the views, the cabin was designed with unusually large windows. As Aspen is fairly southern in location and its winter sun quite strong, the heat coming through the windows more than compensates for any heat lost through the expanses of glass.

🐾 LEFT & ABOVE In winter, residents of this wild spot must get around either on skis or by snowcat, as the only way in by vehicle is via an old dirt track once used by the miners who lived here. However, the area's inaccessibility has kept it beautifully pristine.

# NATIVE HABITAT

C urled like a giant nautilus shell on the snowy fringes of Aspen's Buttermilk run is the extraordinary house of Peter and Patricia Findlay. It is a wholly organic structure in both its layout and materials. Built mostly from Colorado moss-rock and wood, the house is set into the earth so that from certain angles it appears virtually imbedded in it, completely at one with the open land around it. Inside, all the rooms sweep into a central open space that rises through the three levels of the house. There are no rendered walls or conventional building treatments. All the surfaces are left rough and raw and spaces simply flow one into the other.

The highly unconventional design and execution of the house were what drew the Findlays to it when they came to Aspen looking for a holiday home. After scouring the town without finding what they wanted, they saw the property advertised accompanied by photographs only of the expansive views it commanded. Their curiosity piqued, they persuaded a reluctant estate agent to show it to them, despite her best efforts to convince them it would be a waste of time. It was precisely because the house was so unusual that it had failed to attract buyers in the past, having been on the market for several years. The Findlays, however, immediately appreciated its individual character and decided it was a treasure worth owning. They saw it not only as a wonderful example of organic architecture, but also as a slice of Aspen's modern history.

RIGHT The downstairs sitting room is lined in riverbed stone. Low-level seating is clustered beside a massive fireplace which generates an enormous amount of heat. An old pair of snowshoes hangs on one wall.

OPPOSITE All of the materials used to build the house were found in the area. Much of the timber was from the old mine shafts around Aspen, while stones came from the riverbed. The house was constructed almost single-handedly by its visionary creator.

The house is a shrine to 1970s counterculture, so much so that it is known to everyone locally as 'the magic mushroom house' in reference to the magic mushrooms to which its original owner was apparently partial. He was one of many who came to Aspen in the 1960s and 1970s in search of an alternative lifestyle and a creative environment in tune with nature. He set his mind to building his own house, with his own hands, using materials he found in the region. He hauled stone from the river to form the basis for his hippie haven and delved down into old mine sites to heave up timber beams, which he used for the roof and for structural and interior details. Furnishings were low and casual, often built-in, in keeping with the style of the decade.

So neatly did all the elements of the house fit together that the Findlays have changed very little about it. Although they have added a few decorative touches of their own here and there, the rest is largely as it was. The circular lounge area, nicknamed 'the love pit', features the original built-in sofa, while the dining room retains the hanging glass light fittings made especially for it in the 1970s. Fireplaces and randomly placed stained-glass windows have all stayed intact.

Most spectacularly of all, the master bedroom has been kept as its creator intended: a giant circular waterbed that is fitted to fill almost the whole room, with only a small surrounding ledge providing access. A panel of large windows in the curving exterior wall and a huge skylight overhead mean the sky, stars, trees and mountains can be viewed languidly from bed. No magic mushrooms are needed to make this a truly surreal experience.

OPPOSITE & ABOVE When the Findlays took over the house, it was like a jungle inside, literally dripping with greenery. The couple removed much of it in order to simplify and open up the interior space. They have kept just a few potted palms, ferns and cactuses to give the impression that the house is a living, breathing organism.

ABOVE RIGHT The fireplace in the main living area is constructed from a welded unit suspended inside the stone wall, with vents on each floor to disperse the heat. It is indicative of the alternative approach to living enshrined in the house.

☞ OPPOSITE Reflecting the handsome Victorian exterior, classical architectural devices were used to define the interiors. But rather than apply them in a strictly historical sense, designer Peter Kunz used them within a contemporary, open layout.

# VICTORIAN HERITAGE

Aspen's centre is lined with relics of the town's Victorian past. Facades of red brick or colourfully painted weatherboard, verandas with wrought-iron railings, elegant canopies and stained-glass windows all attest to the silver mining euphoria of the late nineteenth century, and the wealth that came with it. When the town went into decline at the end of the 1890s, many of its buildings suffered a similar fate. Some were left to crumble; others were restored and converted into civic and retail premises that now form the core of the commercial district, giving the town its distinctive architectural profile. Fronting Mill Street stands one Victorian classic that has been renovated to combine retail space, a luxurious private residence and the members-only Caribou Club.

The building was constructed in 1890 as a mercantile store, but in ensuing years was reinvented variously as a mortuary, a hardware store and a boarding house, for which the upstairs level was divided into small cells. By the time it caught the eye of art gallery owner and entrepreneur Harley Baldwin, the building was little more than a ruin. But he saw its potential and set about the long process of restoration. The first consideration was satisfying the rigorous demands of Aspen's Historical Society, which controls all development within the historic centre. Baldwin hired architect Wayne Poulsen and interior designers Peter Kunz and Alan Tanksley, and together they came up with a blueprint to satisfy the Society's strict guidelines.

RIGHT & FAR RIGHT The tastes of art gallery owner Harley Baldwin encompass antique objects with textural beauty. In the formal dining room a pair of late seventeenth-century wood and papier-mâché statues from New Mexico stand at the head of the table, which was fashioned from a sixteenth-century Mogul door.

OPPOSITE A Navajo rug, Indonesian tables and sculptures by Donald Baechler inside, and Bryan Hunt outside add a primitive feel to the serene main bedroom.

The facade was restored to full Victorian splendour with decorative elements used in the mannerist fashion that was popular in the late 1800s. Builders in Aspen then had adapted English Victorian details to suit available materials, usually wood in place of the iron, stone, and varied brick used across the Atlantic. Today the building presents an impressive face to the street with its red brickwork, long veranda and full-length windows. The best aspect though is invisible from the street. The back of the building faces the mountains, offering unhindered views of the snow-covered slopes where owner Baldwin works out on the ski runs most mornings.

Above the retail premises at street level and the basement Caribou Club, Baldwin resides in a spacious penthouse, in which the interior detailing echoes the historic exterior. High ceilings, columns, capitals, arches, trims and mouldings were carefully planned to provide continuity with the exterior style. The layout and choice of furnishings, though, are anything but old-world. The interior space flows from one room to another, with minimal wall division between them. This helps to give an expansive feel to the apartment, and in the living areas provides a gallery-like environment where Baldwin can express his passion for modern art. In the sitting room, pale walls, floors and low-level sofas act as a subdued foil to large modern canvases, sculptural pieces and antique porcelain. Elsewhere, in both the living areas and bedrooms, modern art blends seamlessly with baroque, classical, renaissance and even primitive elements to create a perfectly urbane residence in America's most sophisticated resort.

 LEFT & ABOVE The white walls and mouldings
of the sitting room take their cue from the columned
veranda of the historic exterior. The room's pale colour
scheme creates a neutral backdrop for displaying works
by contemporary artists, including a large canvas by
Elizabeth Murray and sculpture by Bryan Hunt.

ABOVE LEFT & RIGHT A favourite painting by Robert Rauschenberg hangs above a glass-topped console created from a pair of French Empire garden ornaments. On either side of the table are two finely crafted chairs, upholstered in bottle green leather secured with bullet-head nails. Also in the Empire style, the chairs are English Edwardian reproductions, and are part of a set of six bought in London.

RIGHT With the help of interior designer Peter Kunz, Baldwin has brought a touch of urbanity to his Aspen home. Together, they have confidently mixed historical styles with modern art to great effect, as is evident in the hallway. Between two matching Empire-style chairs stands the diminutive figure of a bronze boy by sculptor Donald Baechler. Above him is a painting by Robert Rauschenberg.

# MOUNTAIN MODERNISM

The home of Noelle and Cecil Hernandez is situated on the edge of Aspen's historical West End, a startlingly modern structure that combines a sense of the town's Victorian heritage with organic lines that seem to dip and curve like the backdrop of lake, hills and mountains that is visible from almost all the rooms. More importantly its clean lines, both inside and out, make the house low maintenance as well as aesthetically coherent.

As a construction consultant, Noelle Hernandez had a clear idea of how she wanted the house to be built. Architecturally it needed to include hints of the Victorian building style for which Aspen is renowned. This was not only to satisfy the strict planning regulations that attempt to retain the historical spirit of the town, but also because Noelle felt that the house should be in harmony with its built environment. She also wanted to incorporate the resort's modern archi-tectural influences such as the nearby Bauhaus-designed Aspen Institute. The end result is a perfect synthesis of the two creative impulses. Peaked rooflines alternate with curved, all clad in a French zinc plate from which winter snows slide straight off. The exterior walls are faced with concrete blocks, acid-etched for a softer look, which hold up well to the intense sun.

One of Noelle's few concessions to aesthetics over practicality is the bank of windows that provide a panoramic view of Aspen Mountain from the living room. She wanted the windows to be as expansive as possible without looking too cold and

RIGHT An intimate dining room, sectioned off from the living area by a floating wall, is strikingly furnished with a reproduction Charles Rennie Mackintosh suite.

OPPOSITE A dramatic entrance sets the mood for the rest of the house. Visitors enter down a long corridor lined with maple panelling to find a diminutive grand piano that once graced the HMS *Queen Mary*.

stark, so she encased them in a grid of wooden frames. Inside, the warm tones of pale timbers mark Noelle's influence throughout the house. Maple, in particular, is a favourite and she engaged Colorado craftsmen to create many of the interior elements. The detail in the interiors, though, is Cecil's influence. A keen collector of art, and the household curator, he has decorated the rooms with a feel for the modernist style of the 1920s and 1930s – whether a Rennie Mackintosh suite in the dining room, modern American paintings in the living area, or an Art Deco dresser in the master bedroom.

Although both Noelle and Cecil came to Aspen for different reasons – Noelle for the stimulation of a cultural centre, Cecil for the wide open spaces – both are equally passionate about outdoor sports. Their lives revolve around sporting pursuits. In winter, the couple go snowboarding three or four mornings a week after dropping their children at school. And when fresh powder snow falls everything stops so that the family can sneak in a few runs. In summer, mountain biking and hiking fill the gap until the first snow of the season falls. Even when not out in the great outdoors, the Hernandez do not have to go far to enjoy Aspen's astonishing setting. From the kitchen they see the nature reserve with Smuggler Mountain beyond. Only a sheet of glass separates them from the local wildlife: foxes come in winter and bears in summer to frolic in the back garden, Upstairs, the bedrooms take in views of Aspen Mountain on one side and Red Mountain on the other side. Fittingly, for a family obsessed with the great outdoors, the mountain slopes are the first and final sight of every day.

ABOVE The exterior of the house makes concessions to the Victorian architectural heritage of Aspen yet is firmly rooted in the realm of contemporary design and inspired by construction technology.

LEFT Early twentieth-century works of art from the American West are the only decoration in the minimalist living room – its bold lines and stark white walls designed to echo the dramatic landscape outside. An ingenious gas fireplace is encased behind glass doors.

ABOVE & RIGHT All the maplewood panelling
in the house was expertly crafted by an artisan from
Tabernash, Colorado, whom Noelle Hernandez
met while consulting on a construction project. The long
maple-lined corridor on the ground floor has become
a backdrop for displaying modern works of art. An oil
painting by Deborah Remington hangs at the base of
the stairs, opposite a bronze by Jack Zajac. At the end
of the corridor, a landscape by Loren Mozley hangs
above a Charles Rennie Mackintosh reproduction chair.

# INTERIOR DYNAMIC

It is hard to believe, looking at his present home, that Jack Silverman lived in a small log cabin on the same site for years. He was quite happy with his home but changes to Aspen's strict planning laws prompted him into action. It was time to build a new house before new restrictions made it impossible. The long, narrow lot meant that a conventional building was out of the question. What resulted was a structure shoehorned snugly into the site but designed to give an interior impression of space.

Silverman's house is less than eighteen feet wide, yet the proportions appear more like those of a New York loft than a trailer. There are no interior walls, just partitions that divide the open space under a single roof span reinforced with steel. Lighting is another key aspect of the interior environment and it is wired to maximise and manipulate both the level of light and the illusion of space. To make the most of the limited floor area, Silverman built down, sinking a basement below the ground level. This houses the art studio where he creates limited-edition serigraphs.

At one end of this narrow house an open core carves through each level, flooded with natural light through a wall of windows that Silverman based on those in New York's Grand Central Station. This love of design classics is a recurrent theme in his house, and indeed of every aspect of his life. The house itself is a minor feat of engineering, and its shape is narrow and

OPPOSITE & RIGHT To maximise the amount of light within the narrow house, walls and ceilings were kept pale, clad in maplewood or creamy stucco. In addition, the walls were designed as partitions rather than taken to their full height, and lighting was used judiciously to brighten the interior space.

honed like that of a sleek train engine. This sense of aerodynamics extends to Silverman's personal interests. He is a keen collector, and racer, of vintage motorbikes. When not on loan to museums such as the Guggenheim, the bikes take pride of place in the living room. Cycles, too, are another passion, and a bank of them is suspended above the living room. A Koa surfboard displayed in the living room hints at summers spent surfing in Hawaii, while pairs of cross-country skis indicate Silverman's winter preoccupation. Downhill skiing is also a significant part of the owner's sporting routine. Most winter mornings see him on the nearby slopes of Aspen Mountain for several hours on and off piste.

Curiously for someone obsessed with speed, engineering and motion, Silverman is also fascinated with Native American arts and artefacts. The neutral backdrop of his house provides a showcase for collections of pots, Indian dolls, folkloric objects, totems, paintings and photographs that give a strong sense of the native heritage of the American West. It is an interest that is keenly expressed in Silverman's renowned serigraphs of Native American textiles. These detailed silk-screen renderings on paper are based on his own fine collection of early Pueblo and Navajo blankets and ponchos. They are created in his basement studio and sold to international collectors, galleries and museums, including The British Museum and the Field Museum of Natural History. Despite the apparent conflict between the motorbike racer and artist, it is perhaps apt that both Silverman's motorbikes and serigraphs, which co-exist so comfortably in his home, are considered worthy of museum display.

🐇 **ABOVE & RIGHT** Owner Jack Silverman's love of both sports and art is visible in almost every room, including here in the basement library where sporting objects co-exist with pieces of American folk art. Skiing, cycling and motor-biking are particular interests and Silverman races regularly on his vintage Ducati and Benelli bikes.

**OPPOSITE & LEFT** Silverman does not keep his huge array of cycles in a garage or hall cupboard. Rather he displays them openly, making them a feature of the interior, both in the living room and bedroom.

**BELOW** The open plan of the house, and its narrow dimensions, meant limited room for a kitchen. Tucked in a niche adjoining the living room, the modern, maple-lined kitchen is small but supremely functional, fully utilising the available space.

OPPOSITE Looking out over the Roaring Fork River, which snakes its way through Aspen's North Star Preserve, the house of artist Holly Lueders is designed to harmonise with its environment of snowy mountain wilderness.

# PIONEER SPIRIT

The home of artist and interior designer Holly Lueders pays homage to the spirit of pioneering America. It is not in any way nostalgic; rather, it is the use of raw, rugged materials, and an organic approach to decoration that give the house its character. Poised on the south face of Smuggler Mountain in Aspen's North Star Preserve, surrounded by a snowy wilderness, Lueders' winter retreat blends effortlessly with its environment.

Affectionately dubbed North Star Lodge by its owner, the house is certainly on the scale of a lodge, stretched out across the mountain's foothills, an expansive two-storey structure, capped by four pitched roofs and with a deep veranda running the length of the facade. This expansive outdoor deck serves as Lueders' studio and workroom and even winter mornings are spent out here working on the handcrafted tole trays and ceramics for which she is known.

The exterior and internal structures are of solid logs cut from dead or fallen trees sourced locally and from Yellowstone. Up to eighteen inches thick, these logs provide natural insulation from the elements. They also enable the luxury of picture 'windows, which run from floor to roofline, offering views to the preserve and the Roaring Fork River which cuts through it.

Even inside, the fabric of nature is ever-present: walls lined with bark, a feature wall of lichen rock, chandeliers of elk antlers, and beds from tree branches. Texture is everything in Lueders' domain. She employed decorative artists and artisans to

**RIGHT** The massive logs used to construct the house were hewn from fallen trees in Yellowstone and Vail National Parks. They are so thick that very little in the way of heating is required inside.

**OPPOSITE** Although the family have other homes, they choose to spend the winters here. Most days between January and March find them out cross-country or down-hill skiing. When they stay here during the summer, their energies are channelled into cycling and fishing.

work on almost every aspect of the interior fitting and furniture. When cladding the walls with bark or setting beams or railings, timbers were chosen and placed so that interesting knots or features of the wood would be seen and appreciated.

Comfort and decoration are just as important to Lueders as the rough materials drawn from the mountains around her. This counterpoint gives the house great charm, and reinforces the idea of it as a modern frontier refuge. When early nineteenth-century pioneers to the Wild West built log homes using massive pine trees cut from the woods, they gave them homely touches with colourful quilts, hand-embroidered throws and delicately patterned textiles. In the same vein, Lueders has introduced colour and pattern to make her lodge a place of warmth and natural artfulness.

Ceramics are a key element at North Star Lodge – symbolic perhaps of the meeting between rough and smooth, of the interplay between raw elements and aesthetic concerns that characterise this home. Lueders' passion for the ceramic arts led her to commission special pieces from the Doylestown, Pensylvannia, tileworks of the innovative 1920s collector and ceramicist Henry Mercer, using Mercer's original moulds. In the kitchen, Mercer's tiles of the New World bear images of the folktales and natural world of North and South America. Around the library fireplace, other tiles visually convey the narrative of Rip Van Winkle; the ceramic surfaces smoked and oiled to give them a patina of age. Elsewhere, young tile artisans from all over the country have supplied works for Lueders' paean to American craftsmanship.

**LEFT & ABOVE** Sheltered at its back by Smuggler Mountain, the house is nestled in a suntrap and is bathed in light for most of the day. Holly Lueders uses the terrace as her studio, even in winter. In the event of bad weather, a covered walkway leads from the ground level to ensure safe passage from car to house.

✍ OPPOSITE & ABOVE Throughout the house, the textures of exposed stone and rough wood surfaces are countered by plump sofas, cushions, covered stools and rugs. Decorative tiles are also a key element in the interior design of the main living areas. In the library, reproduction tiles from the Henry Mercer tileworks in Pennsylvania surround the fireplace, telling the story of Rip Van Winkle.

OPPOSITE & BELOW The vast 'great room' is the focus for family life. Lueders set out to create a space where everyone could be together, yet do their own thing. The result is numerous cosy seating areas and alcoves, one containing a backgammon table. A swing hangs from the massive rafters.

RIGHT, ABOVE & BELOW Beautiful and unusual objects are woven into the rugged framework of the house, whether a delicate etched-glass chandelier or a backgammon table with a surface of mosaic tiles.

OPPOSITE & ABOVE The house incorporates eight bedrooms, each with a bed crafted from fallen trees found on the property. In contrast to the gnarled branches that form the bed bases and sculptural bedheads, hand-embroidered spreads and cushions made from Hungarian felted wool provide touches of warmth, colour and comfort.

ABOVE & RIGHT One of two master bedroom suites that Holly Lueders and her husband switch between depending on the season. The walls are lined with bark, which was picked in spring and pressed for six months before being fitted. The fireplace, with its mosaic of wood patterns and textures, is a monument to the craftsmen of the Rocky Mountains and their ability to translate indigenous materials into works of art.

🐇 ABOVE & OPPOSITE A snow-white bedroom that reflects the landscape outside. The bed, like the others in the house, was commissioned from a local artisan to give the illusion that the natural world had found its way inside. In fact, most of the furnishings are handcrafted, including a rustic armchair made from willow.

# Ski Guide

## ST MORITZ

### HOTELS

**Badrutt's Palace Hotel**

CH-7500 St Moritz

tel: 41 81 837 1000

*classic hotel where Alpine*

*tourism began*

**Kulm Hotel**

CH-7500 St Moritz

tel: 41 81 832 1151

*legendary celebrity haunt*

**Suvretta House**

CH-7500 St Moritz

tel: 41 81 832 1132

*charming luxury hotel*

### DINING

**Stüvetta Veglia**

CH-7505 Celerina

tel: 41 81 833 8008

*gourmet Engadine cuisine in*

*a village outside St Moritz*

**Talvo**

CH-7500 St Moritz

tel: 41 81 833 4455

*excellent food served in a*

*seventeenth-century mansion*

**La Marmite**

CH-7500 Corviglia

tel: 41 81 833 6355

*best place for lunch*

*on the ski slopes*

### SKIING

**Ski Engadin**

Via Grevas 6

tel: 41 81 830 0000

*ski safaris, winter rambles, lift*

*passes and slope information*

**La Fainera**

Sils Maria

tel: 41 81 826 5502

*ski fashion, ski equipment*

*and rentals*

# GSTAAD

## HOTELS

**Grand Hotel Park**

CH-3780 Gstaad

tel: 41 33 748 9800

*luxurious hotel and spa*

## DINING

**La Bagatelle**

Le Grand Chalet, Gstaad

tel: 41 33 748 7676

*gourmet restaurant*

**Restaurant Chlösterli**

Grund bei Gstaad

tel: 41 33 755 1912

*homemade Swiss specialities*

## SKIING

**Alpinzentrum Gstaad**

CH-3780 Gstaad

tel: 41 33 722 4006

*ski sports and snowshoeing*

# KLOSTERS

## HOTEL

**Chesa Grischuna**

Bahnhofstrasse 12

tel: 41 81 422 2222

*charming private hotel*

*with excellent restaurant*

## DINING

**Rustico**

Landstrasse 194

tel: 41 81 422 1212

*fine seasonal menu*

**Restaurant Alte Poste**

Aueja

tel: 41 81 422 1716

*family-run with Swiss specialities*

**Walserhof**

Landstrasse 141

tel: 41 81 410 2929

*renowned restaurant within*

*a small, elegant hotel*

**Wynegg**

Landstrasse 206

tel: 41 81 422 1340

*rustic atmosphere, regional*

*home cooking and fondue*

## SKIING

**Swiss Ski School Klosters**

Landstrasse 26

tel: 41 81 410 2028

*instruction and guides for skiing,*

*snowboarding, snowshoe treks*

**Hartmann**

Landstrasse 201

tel: 41 81 422 1270

*wide selection of sports*

*clothing and equipment*

# CORTINA D'AMPEZZO

## HOTELS

### Cristallo

Via Menardi 42

tel: 39 0436 4281

*luxurious accommodation*

### De la Poste

Piazza Roma 14

tel: 39 0436 4271

*characterful historic hotel*

## DINING

### Lago Scin

Strada Statale

tel: 39 0436 2391

*famous for its local fare*

### Ristorante Ospitale

loc. Ospitale

tel: 39 0436 4585

*speciality speck dishes*

### Il Meloncino

Gilardon

tel: 39 0436 61043

*famous lunch spot on*

*the ski slopes*

### El Toulà

Ronco 124

tel: 39 0436 3339

*restaurant in a traditional chalet,*

*serving excellent regional dishes*

### Lago Ghedina

Lago Ghedina 2

tel: 39 0436 860 876

*Veneto specialities in a lakeside*

*chalet with waterfront terrace*

## SKIING

### Scuola Sci Cortina

Corso Italia 69

tel: 39 0436 2911

*one of the best ski schools,*

*offering tuition at all levels*

## SPECIALITIES

### Giacobbi

Corso Italia 101

tel: 39 0436 4308

*for Ampezzano and*

*Tyrolean costumes*

### Zardini Stufe

Brite de Val 2

tel: 39 0436 4650

*for traditional ceramic stoves*

### Art House

Corso Italia 96

tel: 39 0436 863 898

*for regional art, antiques*

*and handicrafts*

# ASPEN

## HOTELS

### Hotel Jerome

330 East Main Street

tel: 1 970 920 1000

*historic luxury hotel built in*

*Victorian style in 1889, with*

*ballroom, bar and restaurants*

### The Little Nell

675 E. Durant Avenue

tel: 1 970 920 6330

*outstanding boutique hotel*

*with elegant American-Alpine*

*restaurant and bar*

## DINING

### Caribou Club

411 E. Hopkins Avenue

tel: 1 970 925 2929

*chic members-only club (pictured*

*opposite) with dining, dancing,*

*wine cellar and cigar room*

### Campo de Fiori

205 S. Mill Street

tel: 1 970 920 7717

*Northern Italian trattoria*

*with rustic atmosphere*

### Little Annie's

517 E. Hyman Avenue

tel: 1 970 920 1490

*Aspenites' favourite local*

*restaurant and bar*

### Krabloonik

Snowmass Mountain

tel: 1 970 923 3953

*Wild game and fine wines*

*on the Snowmass slopes*

## SKIING

### Aspen Skiing Company

P.O. Box 1248

Aspen, CO 81612

tel: 1 970 925 1220

*arranges all types of skiing trips*

## SPECIALITIES

### Baldwin Gallery

209 South Galena Street

tel: 970 920 9797

*leading contemporary*

*art gallery*

### Silverman Museum Collection

www.silvermanmuseum.com

*serigraphs of American Indian*

*textiles by artist Jack Silverman,*

*available via the net*

### Aspen Potters

231 E. Main Street

tel: 1 970 925 8726

*stoneware and pottery*

*by local Aspen artists*

### Aspen Santa Fe Trail

205 S. Mill Street

tel: 1 970 925 7022

*American country furnishings in*

*leather, wood, antler and iron*

# INDEX

Note: references in *italics* are to captions.

# Acknowledgments

The publishers thank all those who graciously allowed their homes to be photographed, and regret that not all the homes could be included. For their kind assistance the author and publishers also gratefully thank: Wayne Poulsen, Bianca Vincenzini, Harley Baldwin, Peter Kunz, Holly Lueders, Peter and Patricia Findlay, Cecil and Noelle Hernandez, Jack Silverman, Antonia Zurcker, Maureen McDonald at Aspen Skiing Company, Janet O'Grady at Aspen magazine, Arnd Küchel, Bettina Müller, Leonardo Mondadori, Verde Visconti, Federica Sessa, Gunter and Mirja Sachs, Prince and Princess Vittorio Emanuele di Savoia, Claude Reyren, Giampiero Dotti, Ginevrá Cavalletti, Countess Anne d'Asche, Marquess and Marchioness Emanuele Carrassi del Villar, Eva Beckwith, Sonya Knapp, Claudine Pereira, Janet Fiahlo, Rosita Pesenti, Renata Andreatta, Daniela Leusch, Roberto Memmo, Allegra Getzel, Barbara Guler, Alda Fendi, Patrizia Nave, Roberto Cardassi, Nicole Hermenjat, Jan Brucker, Mason Beekley.

Vintage ski posters, below, from left to right: St Moritz (page 8), anonymous, c. 1950, courtesy of Christie's; Cortina (page 94) by Franz Lenhart, c. 1935, courtesy of Christie's; Fred Iselin Ski School, Aspen (page 146) by Garth Williams, c 1966, courtesy of Mason Beekley at the American Ski Heritage Museum. Additional posters: All Winter Joys (page 99) by Franz Lenhart, c. 1955, courtesy of Christie's; Davos Parsenn (page 208) by Leo Keck, c. 1940, courtesy of Christie's. Photograph page 7: view from the terrace of Antonia Zurcker's Aspen ranch. Additional photographs: © Robert Capa, Magnum Photos Inc., cover, pages 11(r), 12; courtesy Chesa Grischuna hotel, pages 11(l), 13; courtesy Bianca Vincenzini, pages 97, 98; © Margaret Durrance, pages 149, 150, 151.